Contributing

Adrian McAnarney

Emma Mullen

Jo Liddell

Karen Keenan

Lee Clark

Lily Goretzki

Rich Adams

Sarah Jane McGeown

Tabby Kerwin

About this Book

This book is a collection of stories from a group of strangers who became friends on their epic climb of Mount Kilimanjaro in Tanzania in 2023.

The world's highest freestanding mountain, Kili is a test in both mental and physical strength. An adventure that gave us the highest of highs and lowest of lows but at the heart of everyone's experience was the power of connection; to people and nature.

What you read before you leave for Kili is not an accurate representation of the reality and difficulty of the challenge – words cannot really describe it.

These stories are the honest, lived experiences of real people who took on the mountain and all her challenges for both an experience of a lifetime and to raise valuable funds for an array of well-deserving charities. The stories will leave you full of inspiration, respect and maybe a motivation to tread the same path.

Memories
from the Mountain:

The life-changing stories from real people that climbed
Mount Kilimanjaro

First published by Mode for... Publishing in 2024

www.modefor.co.uk

With thanks to all the amazing tour guides, porters, cooks and staff we met in Tanzania that made this trip safe, enjoyable and full of memories to share.

With thanks also to all our amazing group of new friends who helped to sing and support our way to the summit. Our connection will be forever bonded by the power of Kili.

Always remember... *"Pole, Pole!"*

Tabby Kerwin
www.modefor.co.uk

The Kilimanjaro Song

(the song that our guides sang with such hope and motivation on the side of the mountain)

Jambo, jambo Bwana (Hello, hello Sir)

Habari gani (How are you?)

Mzuri sana (Very fine)

Wageni, mwakaribishwa (Foreigners, you're welcome)

Kilimanjaro, hakuna matata (Kilimanjaro, there is no problem)

Tembea pole pole, hakuna matata (Walk slowly, slowly, no problem)

Utafika salama, hakuna matata (You'll get there safe, no problem)

Kunywa maji mengi, hakuna matata (Drink plenty of water, no problem)

Overwhelming, Magical and Breathtaking
by Adrian McAnarney

My interest in hiking the mountains started approximately six years ago when I went to hike in the Mourne Mountains in Co. Down, Northern Ireland. I was instantly addicted to the surrounding beauty and the challenge it gave me.

With these being my local mountains and approximately 35 minutes away by car, I found myself visiting them on a weekly basis. As time went on, and I got more familiar with the mountains, I would start and finish my hikes at different access areas of the mountains, whilst at the same time increasing the challenge and amount of peaks I could hike in a day.

This inspired me to start looking at the possibility of trekking/climbing high altitude mountains. As time went on I found myself watching more and more videos of the mountains in Nepal, Russia and Africa, researching different guide companies, the equipment needed, expenditure and other considerations.
I knew it was only a matter of time before I was booking a trip to one of these locations. The two mountains which I first wanted to climb were Kilimanjaro or Everest base camp.

In February 2023 on a hike in the Mourne Mountains I met a group of fellow hikers. As we hiked up the mountain we began chatting and they said they were doing a trek to Mount Kilimanjaro in September 2023. As this was a mountain I was hoping to climb, and after hearing from the group that there were still places available on this trip, I decided I would join them and signed up for the challenge and self-funded the trip.

The group had already started their own fundraising for the local hospice so I agreed I would help out. I was excited about the trip and intensified my training, taking on further challenges such as the Mourne 7 7s and the Mourne 7 summits—7 summits over 700m high on a 30k circular route of the Mournes.

As the months progressed I continued the training on a weekly basis. I researched my kit for the trip and got all my vaccinations and Diamox (altitude tablets), keeping regular contact with the group as the trip got closer.

On the morning of the trip our group of 10 flew from Belfast to Heathrow and joined the remaining 28 people in our group. There was a great sense of excitement of what lay ahead and from London we flew to Ethiopia before a flight to Tanzania. On the flight to Tanzania I got my first glimpse of Kilimanjaro with its summit high above the clouds. I could feel a rush of adrenalin of what I was about to experience in the following days and there was a sense of excitement in the group. On our bus journey to the hotel we passed through several villages and it seemed so far removed from the life I had left 24 hours ago.

I settled into the hotel that night and we had our official briefing. The following morning, I started my trek from Machame Gate to Machame Camp—our first camp—a 9k, 5-7 hour trek. Excitement of what lay ahead was evident as I took in my surroundings. As I arrived at Machame Camp everyone was happy - day 1 of trek completed. It was time to take in our surroundings and settle into camp life for the next eight days. It was then time for tea, and change out of our hiking clothes, a quick wash or as the guides call it: *"washy washy"*, and organise our kit in the tent. As we all sat for our evening meal in the dining tent chatting to our new trekking friends, we shared stories and got to know each other before settling into our tents and into our sleeping bags trying to get as much sleep as we could. This would be my daily routine for the rest of the trip.

After breakfast the next morning we started our second day of trekking—I was amazed by the amount of porters and all the camp equipment they carried up the mountains. It is unbelievable the amazing job they do on a daily basis which they do with a smile on their faces and a Swahili greeting of:

Jambo -hello

Jambo bwana - hello sir

Hakuna matata - no trouble/ no worries

Such friendly people and nothing was ever too much trouble. These greetings would be repeated on a daily basis throughout the trip.

As we trekked on and arrived at our second camp—Shira Camp—day two was complete. After carrying out our daily routine of washing and dining we were treated to some Swahili songs by the porters and guides. It was a really joyous party atmosphere with everyone singing and dancing; a great end to the day.

We trekked up the mountain in the following days the landscape in front of me was dramatically changing. We were trekking through a diverse range of eco-systems - Savannah, cloud forest, moorland and alpine desert - these were all unique. Some of my highlights going through these eco-systems were Lava Tower and the scramble on the Baranco Wall which added to the trek. As we climbed up the mountain we approached Barafu Camp—this was going to be our last camp before we started our trek to the summit of Uhuru Peak, Kilimanjaro, later that night.

After lunch and a chat with our trekking friends it was time to get into our tents and sleeping bags and get as much rest as we could. Before I knew it, it was time to get up.

This was it...the night I had been waiting for. I was getting very excited and as I put all my layers and head torch on I was very excited about reaching the summit.

As we started trekking off at 11.30 pm the temperature was around -18 degrees. I could feel the cold on my face. I looked far ahead in the distance and all I could see was a line of headtorches like stars shining in the dark. As we trekked up the mountain the line of head torches seemed to go on and on, it was never-ending. The guides on the mountain were great and all I could hear from them was what sounded like a tribal chant—"*wakey wakey ...no sleepy...more fire...more water...pole pole.... pole pole.*"

This continuous chanting, shouting, whistling and singing from different parts of the mountain motivated me and fired me up. This continued throughout the night and with all the headtorch lights up the mountain made it a magical, atmospheric experience, something I will never forget. As time went on and sunrise approached I could see an orange glow on the horizon which was breathtaking.

I could feel the excitement growing as it got brighter. I would soon be at Stella Point a major milestone on summit night. I had read about it and watched videos of this landmark and knew I wasn't far away from the summit. As we trekked on towards the summit the excitement was growing, the views were breathtaking, the glacier and clouds below me and a blue sky and sun above. I could see the summit in the distance, this give me a real lift and a renewed energy level.

As I trekked the final few metres, finally I was at the summit of Mount Kilimanjaro - Uhuru Peak- the highest freestanding mountain in the world at 5895m. I felt in disbelief that I was finally here and had achieved this. It was a surreal feeling and after taking it all in and congratulating each other on this fantastic achievement many photos were taken to capture this precious moment.

After 20-30 minutes it was time to make our descent down the mountain and back to camp. Getting back into camp that evening felt so good after a long 13 hours trekking.

I was so happy but very tired, time to relax and get something to eat. Afterwards I received my Kilimanjaro medal which I was very proud of. There was a great buzz in camp with lots of chat about our day... and soon it was time for bed.

The following morning after breakfast we started our trek down the mountain to Mweka Gate. This was our finishing point of our Kilimanjaro trek. Arriving at Mweka gate I felt very proud of what I had achieved. At the Gate I said my goodbyes to the porters and guides and made my bus journey back to the hotel stopping for some souvenir shopping on the way.

Back at the hotel we relaxed and got ready for our celebration night. This was a great night full of good food, good music, dancing and a real celebration party atmosphere and on waking on the final morning I received my Kilimanjaro certificate before making the long journey home.

Looking back on my trip, I have some great memories, many of which shared with my tent-mate and I have made lifelong friends.

My three top memories of the trip would be:

- the Summit night
- the scramble on the Baranco Wall
- the celebration night

Despite altitude being one of my biggest concerns prior to the climb and having prepared myself for the potential issues of this, fortunately I had no problems regarding this throughout the trip and didn't require the Diamox (altitude tablets).

One piece of advice I would give to someone considering climbing Mount Kilimanjaro is that research is key. Read up and watch videos on the Kilimanjaro Experience; this will provide you with an insight of what to expect on your trip.

If I had just three words to describe my experience they would be...

Overwhelming, Magical and Breathtaking.

Adrian McAnarney

How Can You? How Do You?
by Emma Mullen

Kilimanjaro. I'm two months back and to look at me, you wouldn't think anything has changed. All appears the same, apart from a hidden fridge magnet that says *"I climbed Kilimanjaro"* and some new vocabulary! Sentence openers like *"this one time, on Kilimanjaro..."* slips out every now and again!

I'm two months back and beneath the surface there is the identity of being in my life back home, alongside the identity that I summited the highest freestanding mountain in the world which continues to fight for space to reside within my body, mind and spirit. It's almost unbelievable really!

I'm from a small village in Northern Ireland—Killean, with a population of 75 people according to the 2001 census! I grew up on the foothills of the highest mountain in my county—**Slieve Gullion**, towering 589m above me! I now live with my new reality that I climbed a mountain 10 times its height at 5893m, which took three full days of hiking before I even saw the top!

I'm a mum of two boys and daily my mind drifts from the mundane-ness of sitting in the daily traffic jam on the way to school, past the golden McDonald's arches and the blurred tail lights skewed by the rain battering my windscreen, to *"I have summited a mountain in -17 degrees!"* and *"I know a place far away from this... far from noise and traffic, and lights, and fast food and fast anything"*.

I'm two months back and thankfully I no longer feel the urge to blurt out in shop queues, or to the waitress in a coffee shop, or to random hikers on my hikes back home "*I climbed Kilimanjaro!*". I've stopped telling people now……because usually that sentence is followed by "*Well…..How was it? What was it like? Was it a good walk?!*"

I began to find myself paralysed by these questions as my mind quickly flashed through catalogues of a life's existence to find some sort of sentence to explain my adventure.

I resolved to '*go-to sentences'* like "*aw, it was class!*" "*trip of a lifetime*", "*Came and went*" ending with "*you have to do it!*" as my mind concluded '*How on earth can one sentence, possibly sum it all up?'*

I guess that explains why I now sound like every Kilimanjaro hiker I have ever spoken to about their trip to Kili "*the trip of a lifetime*". "*There's nothing like it*" "*you'd love it!*".

But, oh my, there is a whole story that could be written about the experience in-between. I could write a self-help book on self-exploration and my self-realisation journey, or a novel on friendship and camaraderie, or a real life reflection on belonging, spirituality and finding inner peace or even an adventure book on climbing the highest free standing mountain in the world! Because Climbing Kilimanjaro... is all of these!

As I sit to write my experience, I am struck by the realisation that 103 people, hikers and crew, did the same Kilimanjaro hike in September 2023. We ate the same food, slept in the same tangerine orange tent, faced the same weather, walked the same route with the same people and yet every story you hear on Kili is going to be a unique one. A personal tale. There is no one story. There is no one way to approach your climb. There is no one way to summit. The only thing that every Kilimanjaro hiker will have in common? It fed our soul, filled us with stories that we will tell for a lifetime... and possibly, maybe, made us a much more interesting dinner guest!

On one of many chats on Kili, a Sherpa said "….*Kilimanjaro calls you, and when it does you won't be able to say no!*" I knew this feeling, just like many who hiked with me. For many long years it was a pipe dream, a hike for *when I win the lotto*. For years my father pleaded for me to climb the mountains closer to home regularly asking "*what's taking you away over there*" and usually ending with "*go speak to your mother*". As I reminded him…I'm 40-years-old!"

But when our local hospice featured in our paper saying they needed support in raising £3.6million to keep running for the year, Kilimanjaro was soon keeping me awake at night and then I knew I had heard her calling! Like the Sherpa said, it was impossible to say no.

After eight months of fundraising, conversations soon turned to the *mountain of greatness* (as Kilimanjaro translates), to talk of clothes to pack for the five different climate zones, food and snacks to pack, vaccinations needed, insurance, solar chargers for topping up mobile phones, bags, boots and tablets and flags for the picture at the summit!

Senseless as they may seem, these considerations do make for the six-day hike to be enjoyable! A bowl of hot water, soap and sweet smelling body lotion after a full day of hiking in dust was like heaven. Fresh socks for each day of the climb felt like hugs for your feet and those four Maple syrup flavoured porridge sachets? Well, they tasted like home!

Solar reflection on our glasses, lip screen for burned lips and the summit coat with 800 fill to keep out the cold -17 degrees…. Frequently I found myself recalling the conversations that led to these luxuries being here with me on Kili….. and deeply thankful they had!

But as much as you aim to plan for the practical elements of Kilimanjaro, nothing prepares you physically, emotionally and mentally. How could it? How could you prepare for families of black-and-white colobus monkeys sitting at the edge of the rainforest at Machame Gate, swinging overhead as you try to find a place to pee!

How could you prepare for porters wrapping your five-day hike bag in tough plastic and continuing each day to throw it on their heads and dash past you in trainers, lugging everything from paraffin canisters to folding tables and chairs, and everything but the kitchen sink, while you dare not moan at carrying a day bag!

How can you prepare for the happy smiles of the crew and their singing and dancing at Shira camp as the sun sets on the side of Kilimanjaro, illuminating the glacier in changing shades of pink and orange or unzipping your warm cocoon on Baranco camp at 5.30am to the most spectacular scenes of clouds below you, like you had just stepped out of an airplane! As you watch dawn break on the glacier of Kilimanjaro holding a tin cup of sweet African coffee as the thin air chills your cheeks!

How can you prepare for remembering childlike feelings of ease, stillness and a lack of worry and huddle and giggle with your new hiking family each afternoon in the dining tent over popcorn, ginger nut biscuits and cups of warm tea...as our crew is busy in preparations for dinner with soft Swahili songs whispering in the wind.

We hiked for four days before reaching Barafu Camp 15,000ft (4600m), the final Base camp before our attempt to the summit. Amidst mornings of packing and unpacking, and days trekking through forest zones, and moon like lava slopes at Lava Tower! How do you prepare for thinning oxygen, and long drop toilets, feeling sunburnt, bunged up by dust, altitude headaches yet bursting with pride, overjoy and elation?

How can you prepare for exhaustion from lack of sleep from the cold for those four days that leaves you walking asleep to the summit, to echoes of men shouting *"Wakey Wakey, don't sleep, keep moving!"* as your body continues to put one foot in front of the other up an almost one mile vertical climb.

How do you prepare for temperatures plummeting to -17 degrees on the summit as you *be bold and bare cold*, layering up as you ascend.

There is no doubt about it—hiking at this temperature is hard work! Two hours into the climb my water bladder froze, leaving me with a hefty block of ice to carry, and only one litre of water to drink for the whole climb that takes almost eight hours. Even with three layers on my bottom half, two pairs of socks, two coats and two under layers, three pairs of gloves, a hat, and a balaclava...I felt cold. Mostly my hands and feet... so much so, that some people use the cup of tea on Stella Point to pour over their hands to gain heat instead of drinking it!

How do you prepare for facing your fears? For digging deep? For challenging your self-belief?

In the darkness of summit night there are no distractions from the voices in your mind or the conversation with your self-will. For more times than I can count, how do you prepare to fight the thoughts that you may join the 35% of 30,000 trekkers who take on Kili each year and never reach *freedom*— Uhuru, the peak of Kilimanjaro.

I thought of why I was doing this and the freezing cold days bucket collecting, the friends who stood beside me and people's encouragement of *"good girls"* as they drop a few pounds in our buckets. I thought of home and hugging my family and the phone call to say I did it! I thought of other heartbreaks and pain and challenges and watched them all dissolve into a puff of smoke and disappear into the lights of Nairobi, in comparison to the challenge I faced now. How can you prepare for that?

How do you prepare for the outpouring of emotion as you allow your tears to fall...hearing the Sherpas shout *"you're almost there, keep going, keep moving, sun's coming"* as you watch those in-front of you finally stop!

How do you prepare for the breakthrough—the light after the darkness, the sun on the horizon as it touches the glaciers of Kilimanjaro in the distance. The scenes of elation as Sherpas and hikers hug and grasp each other in joy, disbelief, ecstasy and euphoria!

How do you prepare for the overwhelming sense of gratitude, thanking God for your body, your mind, your group, your life, this experience, this existence, and every choice and sacrifice that led you to here... *"Mum, that car's letting you out".*

In an instant, my mind snaps back to the daily school run and the golden arches, and the wipers battling the downpour of a wet November morning.

I'm two months back and to look at me, you wouldn't think anything has changed, yet everything has changed! I climbed the mountain of greatness! I've been to the peak of *freedom*—Uhuru! If I can battle that... I can definitely handle the school run!

Emma Mullen

Kilimanjaro and Back Again
By Jo Liddell

Let me try and take you on this journey with me...although I am not sure I can adequately put it into words. We were told on the last night that only the people in the tent with us would ever understand our adventure and it's true. You had to be there to know, but I'll try and give you a glimpse.

One Dream...

But it wasn't really ours! In late 2019 a friend had posted on Facebook that they were thinking of climbing Mount Kilimanjaro and were looking for others to join them. A spur of the moment decision saw myself and my husband, Paul, answering that post. I'm not sure if I was more surprised at myself or Paul as neither of us are hikers or campers or particularly adventurous so this was something very far out of our comfort zone!

The only knowledge we had of Kilimanjaro was seeing it on Comic Relief several years ago when a group of celebrities took on the challenge. I thought if Chris Moyles can do it then so can we!

Unfortunately, COVID came along to spoil our plans so fast forward three years and the original group had all moved on to different things. My husband is in the military and we had all moved to different places at this point, and for various reasons, the only people left still planning to climb were myself and Paul—but once an idea gets in my head it's hard to let go, so we were set on still doing it. We had booked our trip three years prior with Global Adventure Challenges and they had been good enough to let us move it to September 2023, so now we were going to be climbing that mountain with a group of complete strangers.

After three years of delays our adventure was looking unlikely once again when Paul had an injury the month before we were due to go, however, he was determined he could still climb so even though he was hobbling the day we left for the airport, we were on our way!

The day we set off a mixture of excitement, nerves, trepidation and a feeling of surrealism that it was actually happening after so long in the planning came over us. After a long journey it was so nice to get to the hotel and that evening meet the rest of the group as we all shared our first meal together. Everyone was so friendly and there were some great characters amongst us—Lee 'the Farke Knight' standing out very early and Tabby with her little blue cornet (would we love that or hate it early in the morning!).

Little did we know at this point that all these strangers were going to bond over a one-of-a-kind experience.

Feeling excited!

...and so it begins...

Our first early 'wakey wakey' bright and early on the 16th September saw 37 strangers with 90+ guides and porters set off to start their trek up the world's highest free standing mountain. At this point Paul and I had already found a connection with a few members of the group. I had bonded with Tabby whilst getting her to plait my hair on the bus and we had both found a fast connection with Rod and Sally who we would go on to spend much of our Journey with.

The start of our climb didn't happen quickly; we spent a few hours at Machame gate going through kit and bag checks, being amused by monkeys swiping at Chigs' (of Great British Bake Off fame) head and having at least 20 'last' toilet trips before we were on our way—I was not looking forward to peeing behind rocks but I soon got over that in the coming days!

Today was a nice gentle hike through the rain forest lulling us into a false sense of security about what was still to come.

Feeling positive!

When Altitude hits...

Night one in camp for us 'non-campers' was an experience to say the least. Paul didn't sleep at all (however a late night toilet trip rewarded us with the most amazing view of the night sky, being closer to the stars than we'd ever been) and I had maybe an hour so. I can't really say we woke up on this morning but we got up. I immediately felt sick, was it the altitude, lack of sleep or both? My head felt like it was filled with a lead balloon trying to break free and forcing down the porridge was a chore! This morning scared me. If I was feeling this bad already, how was I going to make it through the next five days? Cries of *"saddle-up"* left me little time to feel sorry for myself and we put on our bags and started the day's trek.

The Fall of Mark...

The overriding memory of day two will always be the *Fall of Mark*. At a point in the trek where we had to traverse a narrow ledge, our new friend Mark unfortunately was weighed down by his backpack and fell 15 feet into the valley.

This was the moment that I realised what we were doing was dangerous. Before I had only been thinking about getting to the top, now I was thinking about surviving and for a moment thinking about stopping! Fortunately Mark, although having a deep cut to his head, was OK, but he had to end his climb to go and get stitched up.

This evening the Porters and Guides entertained us with singing and dancing and Tabby played her cornet. It was the boost we all needed after a very hard day. *Feeling Scared!*

Drums continue in my head...

The headache from yesterday proved even worse today and I was worried how I would make it as today would see us reach our highest elevation to date with Lunch at Lava Tower.

'Pole Pole', Swahili for *'Slowly Slowly',* saves the day as I really couldn't do much more. Paul kept me going through the day and a lunch time treat of Chicken and Chips definitely helped.

A group of us had stayed behind the larger part of the team today as a few of us were struggling and Tabby was really worrying me (I'll leave you to read her story) but we all made it to Lava Tower through sheer grit and determination.

The beautiful scenery on the second part of today really helped too, the funniest trees we've ever seen. Paul said this was his favourite day so far but if I'm honest I don't really remember it that well as I was so consumed with the drums in my head. I just kept putting one foot in front of the other hoping for the Ibuprofen to kick in.

Feeling weak!

Beat that Wall...

Today was the day we had all been waiting for as we got to scale the Baranco Wall and I couldn't believe it when I woke up feeling absolutely great.

My headache had miraculously disappeared, and I even quite enjoyed my morning porridge. Was I acclimatising to the altitude? A slow climb was all we could do as every step over a rock left us needing a few minutes to catch our breath. The energy needed to do anything more than just walk is astounding. I think we were all shocked how just getting out of the tent in the morning felt like an hour's workout!

Sally and I shared an emotional moment part way up when we couldn't move out of the way for porters coming passed us - it's funny how emotional Kili makes you and after a few tears we were laughing again.

The descent into a deep valley after the wall followed by the ascent up the other side was not something we had been forewarned of, so came as a bit of a shock— but it had been a good day overall and still headache-free we trundled on up to camp.

Feeling energised!

Last stop before Summit...

Barafu Camp (Ice Camp) was our final camp before the summit attempt. Before I take you on the final leg up the mountain with me, let me tell you some of the things I have forgotten to mention that form part of my memories on Kili.

Daily conversations with different members of the group, making new friends every day. Our Irish singers; the lovely Irish contingent in the group singing their way up the mountain – even if we only got a part of every song when they couldn't remember the words it was still uplifting!

Sally and Rod! Paul and I walked most days with this wonderful couple and I will be forever thankful to Kili for bringing us together. Lee making us all laugh with his antics and Tabby inspiring me to keep going through her own show of strength.

Porter's phrases – *'sippy sippy'*, *'snacky snacky'*, *'don't stop to the top'*, *'one team, one dream'* and not forgetting *'we are not afraid'* which, on first hearing Sally and I both thought they had said *'we are not your friend!'*—that will forever make me chuckle! All of these will live in my memories and bring a smile to my face whenever I think of them. The porters and guides really are unbelievable and without them none of us would have been able to go on this journey at all.

Not only do they carry all our kit bags and food and toilets (I'm unbelievably thankful for the portable camp toilets saving us from the long drops!) but they engage with you and sing and chat and do everything they can to keep your spirits up and get you up the mountain. I remember one guide saying to me at Ice camp: *"Stop thinking about Kili!"* It seemed so odd at first but he was right. If you think too much about her and focus too hard on summiting you forget to enjoy the journey—so it's really important to just be in the moment and only think about *now*.

Riddles and games... One of the guides from Global kept us going with daft riddles and games, it was a great way to take your mind somewhere else. I am not generally an emotional person but when tears were falling on day two, I knew this journey was going to be the challenge of a lifetime with everlasting memories.

Feeling Bonded!

Let's Summit...

Have you ever had those dreams where you are trying to run but you don't get any further—it almost feels like you are running in quicksand?

This was Summit night for me, as I really did think I was in a dream or nightmare and I was pretty much sleep walking the whole way. Seriously, did you know you could be freezing cold, walking up a mountain with loads of people around you, hearing the shouts of the porters and still be falling asleep? You do now as that was me! Each few steps my poles were the only things keeping me upright as my head bobbed and my eyes closed. Only Paul behind me and soft nudges from the porters would get me moving again... and Paul muttering *"why on earth did we pay good money for this torture when we could have gone to Disneyworld!"*

It's pitch black, aside from head torches adorning us all, appearing like hundreds of fireflies shining in a never-ending line up the mountain. For eight gruelling hours the scenery never changed as we fought our way up the never-ending switch backs to the summit, and if I'm honest, I barely remember it.

All I really remember was staring at my feet willing them to keep moving and then suddenly (I say suddenly but it felt like we had been walking for years) we were there! The sun rose, we saw the glaciers and glory of the top of Kilimanjaro and the Uhuru sign was just ahead! 200 metres and we had made it to the summit of Mount Kilimanjaro.

I'd like to say I was euphoric at this point but honestly, I was just relieved and tired and ready to go back down. Ready to never sleep in a tent again, ready to shower under hot water, ready to take off my boots and never put them on again. Ready to be done!

Feeling drained!

Reflections......

It is only now, looking back, that I feel the joy of having achieved something so incredible with the one I love the most and the strangers who became family.

The wonder of what we accomplished together will never cease to amaze me and a part of me will always be on that mountain, singing the song of Kilimanjaro, eating yet another bowl of rice, drinking more water than I thought possible and for a rare time in life just being in the moment without technology, social media or any home comforts and yet finding a very raw and real sense of peace and belonging.

As I said at the beginning, I really think you had to be there to truly understand and I am not sure I will ever find the right words to share the experience, the emotions, the inner struggles and joint camaraderie we all experienced. There were some very hard times on the mountain and it is without a doubt the most difficult thing Paul and I have ever done but, over time those memories of the bad parts fade and the happy memories shine through until you are almost left with the thought of wanting to do it all over again! Almost!

I'll leave you with some words that I feel sum up this adventure.

On the mountain we were cold, but on the mountain we were bold.
One team one dream, now we know what it means.
Bonded through experience those strangers became family.
You are as strong as you let yourself believe.
With the love and encouragement from others you will achieve.
Feeling reminiscent and accomplished!

Fundraising...

It would be daft to do such a challenge and not try to raise some money along the way. Our trip was self-funded so Paul and I decided to try raise money for Motor Neurone Disease (MND) as we both had uncles with this debilitating disease. We were very thankful for every donation keeping us going along the way.

Jo Liddell

My Mountain Goddess
by Karen Keenan

"It's not the mountain we conquer but ourselves." **-** Sir Edmund Hillary - one of the first climbers confirmed to have reached the summit of Mount Everest.

Sir Edmund Hillary was also quoted as saying:
"I will come again and conquer you because as a mountain you can't grow but as a human, I can."

Reading these quotes, I realise that Edmund Hillary learned a lot about himself while off on his expeditions and I am sure he learnt many lessons on each and every one of his journeys, whether that was mountain climbing, travelling or sharing the experiences with others and I am writing here to share some of my own personal lessons and experiences whilst climbing Mount Kilimanjaro—both life lessons and the experience of the mountain itself.

Climbing mountains wasn't always my thing; I took up the hobby in lockdown (like most other people) when having extra time on my hands and wanting to get out into nature. I started climbing a few mountains locally and that branched off into doing some mountain challenges for charity. I had previously lost my dad in 2018 to cancer and I wanted to give back to my local hospice by fundraising for them, so climbing Kilimanjaro seemed right.

We often take on these kind of challenges to get something from them; see how far we can push ourselves and hopefully to change us in some way or learn from it. On reflection here are a few lessons I have learned having climbed one big ass mountain!

Lesson One – Connections

This is not a challenge you can do on your own as when climbing Kilimanjaro you need all the help you can get.

Sometimes it's difficult for me to ask for help and I realised very quickly on this trip that I couldn't do it on my own. Surprisingly (to me) that was such a nice and comforting realisation, especially since there were plenty of people willing to help. I have also seen how strangers can become family in such a short amount of time. You have a sense of vulnerability and you put your trust and confidence into people which creates strong bonds and connections as everything is so intense.

No internet connection left space for even more human connection—small conversations made between people creating a sense of knowing and belonging within each other. Levels of support and encouragement giving a genuine belief and desire that we could all achieve this beautiful mountain together - and as a group of 37 novices we did it - #dreamteam.

Lesson Two – Inner Strength

I made it to the summit!

This shows me that if I really put my mind to something I can do it. You literally question your sanity on that mountain every single day. My two best friends were acceptance and living in the moment, just taking one small step at a time and not thinking too far ahead. You can only think in the present; I closed off thoughts of home and my daughter to make it easier to keep in momentum. The days are long and nights even longer, battling through the effects of altitude and the cold on top of tiredness it really is a war of the mind, and you must keep pushing through. You are so far past the point of your comfort zone that you are making a conscious effort to expand your resiliency and use all your resources both mentally and physically to achieve an incredible win at the end while still asking yourself:

"What am I doing here? Can I do this? I would be better at home. This isn't for me."

Like everything in life the battle wasn't with the mountain, the battle was with myself, fought between my spiritual self and my ego and this time my spiritual self was the winner.

Lesson Three – Accepting Help

As I have already said I don't like asking for help. I try to do as much in my life on my own, even to the extent of self-sabotage and leaving myself worse off. I realise this isn't a positive trait and something I need to heal and work on!

When you are on Mount Kilimanjaro you have no choice but to accept help and mostly from the guides and porters, who are willing to help as much as possible.

At the beginning I was very resistant to this but very soon I realised it could be seen as quite defensive and stand-offish. The guides and porters wanted to help, they were happiest helping people and when I did accept the help it made the experience a little easier for me—it opened up more conversations and connections along the journey with more people. The positive effects of a happy smile, a helping hand an encouraging voice to make you feel supported and safe along the journey will forever be in my heart.

Lesson Four – Digging Deep

Remembering when you have peaked you have the long road back down...

You have nothing left in you at this stage, even breathing is hard! This is survival now, no push or drive left, your whole body just wants to rest. The main event is done, you are full of frustration, tiredness and fatigue. There is no glory in this last stage - it is down to practicality and finding the determination to get back to camp, there is no easy way out, it's just one foot in front of the other and this is still part of the journey.

The mountain is just like life; when you go up you must come down. In climbing this mountain I learnt it is like walking through life—the ups, the downs and all the in between bits. I've a new appreciation for my own life now and who I call friends and family. I hope to take all these lessons and live them within myself. It is the gifts of spirituality, belonging, persistence and feeling the fear but just keep going anyway.

Mount Kilimanjaro, like the many other mountains I have climbed have become a place of retreat for me. A way of tuning out, connecting with something else indescribable, something of spiritualty and beauty, away from the bustling noises of towns and cities and the rat race of life for a while.

Connecting with the mountain and with nature, it finds a way of connecting with your inner-self. Seeing the magnitude of a mountain and how little I am as a human in comparison gives me a sense of grounding and perspective.

"I understood at a very early age that in nature, I felt everything I should feel in church but never did. Walking in the woods, I felt in touch with the universe and with the spirit of the universe." – Alice Walker, American novelist, poet and social activist.

That is how I feel in the mountains and in nature.

Forever my church – Forever my home.

Kilimanjaro is my mountain goddess.

Karen Keenan

The Longest Summit Night
by Lee Clark

After numerous other fundraising challenges including football matches, sponsored silences and climbing the National Three Peaks a few years ago, the idea of climbing Mount Kilimanjaro came up randomly in conversation. I didn't even know what Kilimanjaro was, but with a mission to raise £1 million for charity by the time I'm 60-years-old, the challenge was on.

I really enjoyed the National Three Peaks challenge—it was an escape from the real world—and I trained so hard for it, losing seven stone in weight. I was driven by the thought that I didn't want to let any of my sponsors down who were donating to the charity and the driver was the same for Kilimanjaro, so I really committed to my training.

On speaking to anyone who plans to climb Kilimanjaro I would absolutely recommend training by yourself.

I did this, training walking up and down steps for hours and this training on my own helped prepare me mentally and physically because you have to be comfortable in your own head. Prepare for the worst and the hardest challenge, train on your own and when you don't feel like doing any more training, when you're a bit tired, push a little more. It was this training that really helped me, especially when it came to summit night when the challenge got even harder for me.

Even attempting climbing Kilimanjaro is a great success and it's just about you. It's your personal challenge to get there and do yourself proud. You want to walk away from that mountain knowing you gave it your best shot and if you give it your best shot, no one can judge you on that.

The challenge is so big that people don't really mind whether you make it to the top or not. You go at your own pace and you are always surrounded by people who want you to succeed and they all really support you. I made some great friends who supported me on the mountain, especially Sally and Rod Shipley and Jo and Paul Liddell.

All the guides and porters were incredible too and they helped with everything you needed and were with you every step of the way. Everyone is there for you, wanting you to succeed in your personal challenge and there is never any shame if you can't do something. But I was really determined to make it to the top, no matter what it took.

I was scared at the start of the challenge. That first day, when we started climbing up the mountain I was thinking *"this is too fast for me.*
I can't keep up with this. I'm really struggling and this is only day one." I kept having those intrusive thoughts thinking I wasn't' going to make it. But soon the pace slightly changed when Tabby took to the front of the group and I was so grateful for her slower pace. It started to make me believe I could do this and I started to better manage my anxious thoughts.

I was so tired when we got to camp on the first night and so out of breath, but I looked around at everyone else and I saw that they were all tired and struggling too, but we were buzzing we had started and I quickly realised I wasn't the only one feeling this mixture of emotions where it felt so hard but also it was so exciting. Soon my feelings of shame passed and the next few days, whilst difficult, were fun and I got to know the amazing people in our group.

It's a great atmosphere on the mountain. It's a carnival atmosphere sometimes with singing and dancing and you meet so many new people and well-wishers. No one's horrible or rude and I was so grateful for that, especially on summit night.

Summit night was so hard and if it hadn't have been for the amazing porters and guides I never would have made it to the top. I was determined to make it, even though I don't think everyone thought I could. But the porters and guides got me to the top. They were so re-assuring, helping me every step of the way, dragging me along when I needed it.

I remember seeing the lights from the head-torches climbing the mountain, and my speed had dropped so much that some climbers were coming back down the mountain before I had even got to Stella Point; the penultimate break point before the summit.

Eventually I made it to Stella Point and from there it took me another two hours to the summit. It became harder the later in the morning it got as the snow started to melt in the sunshine and gravel became even more slippy. My porter and guide gave me the option to stop at Stella Point and head back down but I was determined to summit so they helped me achieve that and get my photo at the top of the mountain. It had taken me 13 hours, but I eventually summitted and the relief and emotion was immense. I was so tired, but I knew I had to get back to camp, so we started the return journey.

The descent was hard and my guides and porters took it in turns to support and hold me as I made my way down.

We arrived at base camp and the rest of the group had already moved on to our camp for the final night. This was about another four hours further down the mountain and I begged the porters and guides to let me stay at base camp because I was so tired and didn't think I could make it any further. I hadn't seen my group of friends for so long now. They said I couldn't stay at base camp and I would have to keep moving, making my way down the mountain until I reached our final camp for the night.

Eventually I made it – 21 hours after I departed for the summit. I was exhausted, broken but grateful for all the assistance the porters and guides had given me and grateful to see my group. My stubbornness had worked in my favour as I was determined not to let anyone down, especially not the charity I was raising funds for. I was also grateful for the solo training I had done because that allowed me to feel OK about being on my own on that long summit night and day. I was stopping every five minutes but I knew I didn't have to worry about upsetting others around me or slowing their journey. I needed to go at my pace and I was more relaxed and more comfortable knowing I could do that.

I didn't want to fail. I didn't want to let anyone down. I wanted to do my charity and my sponsors proud and I wanted to be proud of myself, and I achieved that. Climbing Kilimanjaro, as challenging as it was, gave me that opportunity.

I was scared and nervous the day I left home for this challenge and flying into Tanzania, seeing the mountain above the clouds the reality of the challenge started to become clear. But driving to the hotel from the airport, seeing the people at the sides of the road and smiling and waving at them made me realise what an amazing country and people they were. It made me feel more confident.

On the day I left Tanzania, as we flew over Kilimanjaro one last time, I felt proud—buzzing at what I and all of our group had achieved and I remember thinking *"I've just been up there! Wow!"*. It was in that moment you realised just how big Kilimanjaro is because when you're climbing the mountain you don't get to see that, because you're on it. But looking down from the plane was just amazing.

Before I undertook this challenge, I didn't understand the enormity of what I was getting myself into. I also didn't know the massive impact that it was going to have on me and the difference it would make on people's lives. The amount of support I got was incredible and in honesty, at first I didn't really realise what I had achieved. I didn't realise how massive it was. I've had people come up to me at work and online who attempted the challenge and hadn't made it and they were incredibly fit. Over time though, the reality has started to sink in and I'm both proud and grateful for the amazing experience I had climbing and summiting Mount Kilimanjaro.

Lee Clark

'Crusing' up Kili
by Lily Goretzki

In September 2020, my Uncle Michael died suddenly after having a cardiac arrest at home—triggered by a seizure. Having seen my family's grief and sorrow, I understand the importance of bereavement support and how widely it is needed, so I climbed Mount Kilimanjaro for Cruse Bereavement Support

My Mum ended up working for the charity and this was how I became aware of the challenge. 'Chigs' (of Great British Bake Off fame) was the charity's ambassador and was going to climb Kilimanjaro so the charity was looking to build a 'Team Cruse' for the trip. Honestly, I really didn't put much thought into why I wanted to do that particular challenge and it was very much more a case of *"why not?".* Knowing the importance of the support Cruse provides gave the perfect reason to do it.

I'd never really done anything similar before—the closest thing was walking holidays in Scotland, which turns out aren't comparable at all! I did a few bigger climbs whilst I was there a couple of months before the challenge, including **Schiehallion** and **Ben Lawers**, and this was the main bulk of my training. I sort of knew that I'd be alright in terms of physical fitness for the climb, so put most of my effort into the fundraising element. The main fundraising event I did was a 50 mile overnight walk with my Dad and brothers from my home in Ely to Thornham Beach in Norfolk; my uncle's favourite beach. En route we had a break at my grandparents' house to rest and refuel. They still live in the house that Uncle Michael, my Mum and their brother Andrew grew up in, and going back there these days always feels poignant. But it wasn't just my grandparents who were there as they had invited loads of village friends along for a cheese and wine fundraising evening, so what we thought was just going to be a stop-off break turned into a small party and a celebration of Uncle Michael. I'd like to say that energised us all for the rest of the walk, but the truth is it was agony—we had massive blisters at the end and my main memory is of my youngest brother lying in the middle of a path saying he couldn't go on; he could!

Despite all the pain, I was still amazingly excited about the far bigger walk on the horizon.

The main thing I remember when telling friends and family that I was going to climb Kilimanjaro was that everyone would ask *'who are you going with?'* and were always a combination of impressed and worried when I just said *'by myself.'* I am so happy I made the decision to do it alone though and feel the interactions with the guides and my fellow climbers were more meaningful to me as I was doing it completely alone. I have absolutely no regrets in going alone, I was a fairly confident person before the trip anyway, but the experience just made me so much more sure of myself and what I am able to achieve.

Weirdly, the bit I was most concerned about was making sure that I had all the equipment on the kit list we were sent before the challenge. It felt like it took forever getting everything together for it. Nothing about the actual climb phased me too much before we left for the trip though and even as the trip got closer, my only worry was the risk of losing my baggage at the airport—and how stuffed I'd be without it!

I never doubted that I would be able to do it. My inspiration was to raise funds in honour of my Uncle, his wife Louise and their two children Lola and Isaac. I did quite a lot of research and watched vlogs before the trip as well, so I feel I was fairly well prepared of what to expect and was able to get excited for bits that I had seen others enjoying.

Meeting my fellow climbers was a bit all over the place as everyone arrived at the airport at different times, so the first time we were collectively together was when we arrived at the hotel. When we were told that the size of our group was 37 people, I remember thinking it would be impossible to learn everyone's name and get to know them as well as the guides, but when you're thrown into spending 24 hours a day together, and cover all sorts of conversation topics you get to know people pretty well—and fast too!

The day we started climbing I was so excited to see the route as we were told the first two days were the best for scenery. This was also the day where I realised how much the porters actually did for us. I had seen pictures online of porters carrying massive bags with all the camping equipment in, but actually witnessing them complete the route with bags balanced on their head walking at four times our speed was incredible - they are your personal superheroes whilst on the mountain.

It's hard to pick favourite moments from the trip but parts that really stick out was the *'party on the side of the mountain'* on night two where the guides and porters started singing and dancing and got all of us to join in. Conquering the Baranco Wall was near enough a day of rock climbing, it was really exciting as it broke up the walking we had been doing for the last 3 days and you really had to be determined to reach the top of the wall. But the obvious highlight was reaching the summit. It's a feeling I'll never forget.

I wasn't really impacted by altitude apart from summit night - it was the hardest night of my life. I was feeling sick due to lack of food and sleep and the climb that night was a gruelling battle uphill. It was pitch black and the only light was from people's headtorches and the stars- I had heard on a podcast that when you look up on summit night you can't tell where the headtorches end and the stars begin and that's 100% true—it's simultaneously a blessing (as you can't see the steep climb ahead) and disheartening (as it looks like it'll never end). I was sick from the altitude about midway through the climb, but this didn't 'ruin' the night at all and was actually the point of the challenge where I appreciated the guides most - they helped me put extra layers on when I was too cold to do so myself, let me borrow their headtorch when the battery in mine froze and constantly gave me and everyone else encouragement.

My plan for summit night had been to have a playlist blasting as a sort of motivation and distraction from the climb; this plan failed when I accidentally looped one song for the entire night - Nick Mulvey's cover of *'Moment of Surrender'* which made me want to surrender and feel like I was going crazy too! Thankfully, my earphones died as we reached Stella Point (the last stopping point before Uhuru Peak) and by then I was just so determined to get to the end. Reaching the summit is massively overwhelming and an emotion that's hard to describe. All I know is that I've never smiled and cried so much at once. It was a bit hectic up there trying to get the perfect summit photo and a lot of pushing in the queue to get to the sign. I was one of the first of the group to make it to the summit and I'm not really sure how long I spent up there; the main memories of the summit are loads of photos and hugs all round.

I found the descent 10 times harder than the ascent. All the determination to make the summit had gone and it got to a point on the final day where I just wanted to reach the finish line. I also found it physically harder as it has been raining below the clouds for the last 2 days and the rainforest track we followed was essentially a mud slide.

I still enjoyed it, but fell over not so elegantly multiple times! I actually really enjoyed being disconnected from the rest of the world whilst on the mountain. Being constantly surrounded by people, I didn't feel like I was missing out on anything socially by not being able to contact people.

The only 'home comfort' that I really missed was being able to shower, especially when it got to the point where dry shampoo and a baby wipe wasn't cutting it anymore. Other than that I didn't really struggle, and I slept better in my sleeping bag than I normally do at home! When we reached Mweka Gate at the end, I wanted to tell my family and friends that I had actually done it, but other than that I didn't want to take my phone off flight mode. I loved not thinking about anything else and just living in the moment.

It's hard to give one piece of advice to someone wanting to climb Kilimanjaro without going into massive amounts of detail, but for practical bits of advice - take a good portable charger, take plenty of pictures and make sure you're comfortable in your walking boots and have enough layers... and on a more cliché note - enjoy it and embrace every moment.

There was a moment on the flight back where you could see Kili above the clouds. That was amazing. Actually climbing the mountain and reaching the summit means you lose a bit of perspective on how big she actually is and seeing it above the clouds made me realise what I'd actually achieved.

Even now, several months on, there isn't a day that I don't think about Kili and I haven't enjoyed anything as much since. When I first came back everything felt so mundane and insignificant in comparison. I now want to climb more mountains in the future and take on as many challenges as I can. Everyone around me knows how much I loved the trip. I mention it at every opportunity I can to the point of being irritating! Now, the memories all sort of merge together a bit, the difficulties of summit night are massively glossed over by the fact it's the best thing I've ever done. No one would even have to attempt to convince me to do it again- it would be a **YES** in a heartbeat.

Lily Goretzki

It's All About the People
by Rich Adams

The challenge of climbing Mount Kilimanjaro was all about people. The people that would benefit from the charity I was supporting, a charity for homeless families in Stoke-On-Trent, the people I hadn't yet met and the people that would guide me safely up to and down from the summit.

Prior to taking on the challenge I didn't know anyone who had climbed Mount Kilimanjaro, so it was an unknown but I wanted a challenge—I didn't want to do something that'd be easy. I was going to do something properly challenging for myself, mentally and physically.

Without knowing anyone who had completed the climb, my expectations were just based on what the information I had been sent from Global Adventure Challenges. Before we started, I found several articles online but nothing more than that. I knew it was going to be difficult. I knew there'd be challenges, potentially with altitude and I knew that if you get altitude sickness, there was no rhyme or reason for why—you were either going to be lucky with it or you're unlucky! That was about all I knew!

That lack of information did lead to some fear though, because I tend to be a planner, so even reading the kit list I was trying to question myself if I needed to take more or less or If I'd bought the right things! For me that was where some of the worries came from—being unprepared.

I think I prepared as best I could though, both physically, mentally and in terms of equipment. My mental preparation was helped massively by the continuous support I had from my wife, daughter, close friends and family. I had a personal trainer help me and give me a programme which he had tailored based on information he got from a friend who had completed Everest Base Camp. I also had a great Physio who helped sort out numerous injuries and niggles I picked up with training. Both of these helped me be as physically prepared as possible and physically I think the challenge met my expectations. But, it's the bits that they don't tell you about before that is hard to prepare for... like the camping! I'm not a camper so I didn't know what to expect so that was probably worse than I was expecting and nothing can prepare you for sleeping on rocks on the side of a mountain like that and every night slipping down the tent, ending up wet at the bottom of it!

The reality of the challenge itself only really hit me when we landed at the airport in Kilimanjaro. It was just chaos at the airport trying to get through and then seeing the bags being thrown onto the top of an old minibus we would travel in. I remember thinking *"if this is disorganised here, then what's it going to be like when I climb the mountain!"*

I'd never been anywhere like that, with that sort of chaos—this was a whole other level and the driving and roads were crazy. I was so glad I wasn't driving on those roads! I don't think anyone realised how much we were taking our lives into our hands sitting in those little buses!

As it turns out, that chaos wasn't reflective of our climb at all and the porters, guides and cooks were so well organised and the most amazing support. They really helped in the highs and lows of the whole trip and there were plenty of highs and lows!

For me, reaching the summit was a huge high point and making it back down safely, although that was one of the hardest points of the whole trip coming back down on summit night. My biggest high point had to be the people though; the friends I made and the joy of the Tanzanian people and their dancing, singing and smiles on the side of the mountain.

The biggest challenge for me was definitely summit night. It was the most emotionally challenging part for me, because it was so long of not being able to talk, because it was just too difficult to talk to anyone. Multiple hours, slowly tracking uphill in the freezing cold in the dark, just with your own thoughts was so emotionally challenging.

I was going on the trip on my own so meeting a group of strangers brought some nerves. I was aware I was doing this on my own; I wasn't going there with anyone. We had had a few odd little comments online in the Facebook group but I didn't know anyone. I was going to be spending seven days on a mountain, doing something quite physically and emotionally challenging at times, with a group of people that I've never met. Thankfully though it was a great group of people and I think that that was a massive high—the group dynamic—how there were lots of different people to talk to who came from lots of different walks of life. Everyone was friendly, approachable, supportive and generally brilliant company. Combining the people with the incredible scenery which went from jungle to desert to snow and ice was amazing – I don't think my photos of the views do it justice though!

One of our group having an accident and having to leave so early on was so devastating for our us all as we had become so close and his accident also highlighted just how dangerous what we were doing actually was. This was a low point for everyone I think because of the camaraderie we had built in our group over a short space of time. We had created such good bonds and relationships in our group and with our porters, cooks and guides. I don't think I would have had so many photos if it wasn't for other people either—there was always someone willing to take a photo so we have the memories and sometimes now when it's quiet I take a moment to look at the photos and reflect at the amazing experience which I'm really proud of. I never thought I'd be able to be in the position to do something like this let alone actually do it.

It's amazing when you realise that whilst things can be difficult you can put your mind to it and achieve them; you can do these things that are physically and mentally challenging. Whilst you maybe think you can't do something, when you put your mind to it then you can.

There was such a feeling of joy crossing the line at the end, knowing that you had arrived with a goal of getting up there. I remember thinking *"I've done that. I've actually been up the world's highest freestanding mountain."* I'd been to the top of it and come back down and it's such a feeling of accomplishment and pride. The only thing I missed in the whole trip was not being able to see that iconic view of Mount Kilimanjaro. Yes, you could see it as you flew in and out but that was only the top of the mountain. I would have loved to see the mountain in its entirety to appreciate the accomplishment even more.

Reflecting on the whole trip I can describe it as being ***challenging, uncomfortable and fulfilling***. I'd advise anyone thinking about it to do it—you'll not regret it... just make sure you train for it!

Since my experience last year my perception of the trip hasn't changed. It still feels so surreal but I'm proud; proud that I managed to do it and proud that I just took the plunge and booked it in the first place and said *"right, yeah, enough, I'm just going to go and, and do it."* Would I do it again though? The answer is **NO!** But that's only because there are so many other challenges I want to attempt... next stop Everest Base Camp hopefully... for one thing, it doesn't involve tents!

Rich Adams

From Glasgow to Growth
by Sarah Jane McGeown

Why Mount Kilimanjaro?

"I'm going to climb Kilimanjaro—what do you think?"
This was my friend Lisa to me in September 2022.

"I'm in! 100%". Me, immediately!

I can only assume climbing Mount Kilimanjaro is at the top of many bucket lists around the world, but I never had any ambition to stand on the **'Roof of Africa'.** I don't even have a bucket list! I do something else. I say yes to experiences that give me the opportunity to grow and learn and to connect with others, even when I haven't been expecting those opportunities.

These experiences often come with pain, discomfort, stress and emotions but I've come to realise so much good can be hidden behind struggle. I firmly believe if you're open to life and new experiences, life will lead you to the most interesting places—including the highest free-standing mountain in the world.

I also love to hike. I'm at my most grounded and peaceful when I'm outdoors on the hills. I love the sense of freedom that comes from hiking, forced to be present and experience the world around me.

This challenge also felt right because it was a chance to give something back to my hometown and raise money for a charity that impacts the lives of the people of Armagh who are living with life-limiting illnesses. I'd known of the Southern Area Services Hospice and wanted to support their mission but it was only when I started fundraising for them that I fully understood their importance and presence in the community.

At fundraising events, people would share stories of their loved ones and the incredible care and support they received from the Hospice, often with tears in their eyes and a smile on their face. There is so much love and gratitude when people talk about the Hospice. These stories drove me to fundraise more and to train harder and I knew they would keep me going if I ever felt like I was struggling along the way, before, during and after the climb.

There were nine of us in the group raising funds for this charity and by September 2023, just before the challenge, we had raised over £47,500. An amount that was beyond all our expectations. Each person had to raise a minimum of £5000. And without the help and support of my family and friends, my sister Joanne in particular, I would have struggled to reach that target alone. In the end I raised over £6400. Now, all we had to do was complete the climb.

Getting to Tanzania

I started my journey at Glasgow Central station on Thursday 14 September 2023. I made my way to London Heathrow to meet the rest of the group before we boarded our first flight to Addis Ababa Bole International Airport.

Excitement levels were high with something of a state of disbelief lingering - was this actually happening? Like many in the group this trip had consumed me. I had spent the last year thinking about it, dreaming about it, fundraising, planning and packing. I had spent many weekends in the beautiful and wild Scottish hills training for it...
and now it was finally here.

We landed in Tanzania the next day. We made our way to the bus outside (thankfully with all our luggage!) and you could instantly feel the hot African sun. The local guides strapped our bags to the roof of the bus while I jumped on and purposely grabbed a window seat.

This was my first time in Africa and I didn't want to miss a thing! I stared out the window in awe whilst we drove through large farmland and small, busy villages. Spotting local women carrying huge baskets on their heads effortlessly while young children waved at us as we passed. I felt incredibly blessed to be sitting on that bus.

We arrived at our hotel and met the rest of our group. There were 37 of us; a mixed bag of Irish, Scottish, English and American climbers. By the end of the ten days we would be like family.

At first I (nervously) thought *"this is a lot of people trying to get up this mountain. Is this going to be crowded or stressful?"* I didn't see the advantage in such a large group but within the first day, I realised there is strength in numbers. These people would become my support system; a stable source of kindness, laughter, and motivation. That connection is what got me up that mountain.

And so it begins...

Well rested and fuelled up, we left the hotel early on 16 September and made our way to Machame Gate—our starting point. At the gate, we signed in to the National Park to record our presence and to ensure we would receive our completion certificate at the end of the hike.

It was a big book, with the names of past fellow hikers who'd had the same dream as me; *get to the top*! We had some food and waited while the guides sorted our luggage with the porters.

This was a huge operation: all our baggage, food and equipment was divided up between 90 staff. I didn't expect that amount of help but we needed each and every one of them to get us through this challenge and to reach the summit and back
down again safely.

Just as we began trekking through the rainforest we saw blue monkeys. One in particular got up close and personal to a member of our group, cheekily on the hunt for food, while others swung in the trees. This was my first time seeing monkeys in their natural habitat which initially flooded me with fear but (once I hid my snacks!) I relaxed and enjoyed observing them. The first of many remarkable moments on this beautiful mountain.

The journey up the mountain

The first two days of the trek were challenging but bearable. You quickly get into the routine of being on the mountain.

Every morning was the same - a 6am start with coffee in the tents, then we would get dressed, repack our bags and have breakfast. Before we were fed, I would take a small wander around the camp and find a spot to sit and take it all in, appreciating the incredible views – we were now above the clouds.

Most mornings we would start trekking at 7am and walk for six or seven hours with occasional breaks. So many great stories were shared and songs from every decade were sung. It was during these long days I made strong friendships; friendships that will last a lifetime. Then we would reach camp, our home for the night, relieved but equally overwhelmed by the breathtaking views so remarkably different from that of the camp before. We would eat dinner around 6.30pm followed by a briefing on what to expect the next day. By then, it would be dark and we needed our head torches to navigate around the camp. I loved nighttime on the mountain. With clear views of the Milky Way, constellations and planets, it was simply out of this world (pardon the pun!). I saw my first shooting star on Kilimanjaro.

Just as we arrived at Shira Cave Camp on day two we received the devastating news that a group member had fallen along the route. It was a tricky walk with some exposure and sections of rocky scrambling and Mark had tripped and fallen 15 feet head first. He had to leave the mountain immediately and seek medical assistance at the local hospital which was nine hours away. Because of the severity of a head injury especially at high altitude, it was too risky for Mark to continue.

It was only the second day of our journey and I had only just met Mark, but he was already part of the family we were building and I felt incredibly sad we were losing him. His exit made me realise this dream, goal, experience — whatever you want to call it — was also dangerous, not to be taken lightly and could be over very quickly. Mark said he would come back and finish the climb someday; I really hope he does.

That evening, spirits were lifted by our incredible team. The 90 guides and porters came together and performed local songs which offered an amazing insight into their culture. Everyone was beaming with positivity, laughter and energy. Together, we danced, clapped our hands and connected until the sun began to set. It was exactly what everyone needed. Once we got our breath back (dancing at 3,810m is tough!) we were gifted with the most divine sunset surrounded by a blanket of clouds. We gathered to admire it before we were called for dinner.

That second day really did confirm what I'd anticipated: Kilimanjaro is a rollercoaster of emotions. You feel it all. The emotions that ran through me during my time on the mountain were strong and often inexplicable. Walking along either mid-conversation or on my own, I would feel a strong overwhelming rush of heat move through my body that would leave tears rolling down my face.

It's hard to know exactly why this happened or what it was. Maybe it was the reality of what I was doing, how far I'd come, the beauty around me, the support and connection I'd made with the group and the porters. Maybe that's what true gratitude feels like.

As we entered day three, the latter stages of the ascent, the temperature dropped significantly and the altitude symptoms began to affect most of the group with severe headaches, stomach cramps and difficulty breathing. We took a break at Lava Tower (elevation 4,627m) and in the last 20 minutes of the trek I felt a difference in my ability to move. It was a strange feeling that had no build up but came over me all at once. My body became heavier and every step felt tough.

When I stopped at the top, I felt light headed, but only for a few minutes. We rested, hydrated and ate lunch at Lava Tower to allow our bodies to adjust to the changing conditions. It did help, I shortly felt fine, and we then descended to Barranco Camp for the night at an elevation of 3,950m. The golden altitude rule:

"walk high, sleep low".

On day four, we started our trek on the rocky slopes of the Barranco Wall. This was undoubtedly the most challenging and exciting part of the trek so far. The steep and narrow path at times required me to scramble on all fours to navigate to the top. Along the route, you reach a section known as the kissing wall — as you hug the wall to avoid falling off a steep drop, you traditionally kiss the wall as well. And I am not one for breaking traditions....

The start of day five was a short but steep trek across a dusty, barren landscape. We arrived early at Barafu Camp (elevation of 4,673m), the last camp and resting point before the summit. I cried when we arrived at the camp. I was overwhelmed but these were happy tears. I was so proud of myself; of everyone. We had made it.

The camp was very busy and the weather was extremely changeable, shifting from hot and bright to freezing and wild, high winds.

I'm no stranger to wild weather living in Scotland but this weather was different. It felt unsafe. There was so much dust flying around, making it hard to see and breathe. The rest of the day I spent in my tent protecting myself from the weather and trying to sleep before having an early dinner. I think I closed my eyes for ten minutes. It was incredibly difficult to sleep with the altitude, the excitement... and the nerves. The summit was near.

Summit night

The time had arrived. The moment we had been working towards the last five days. Summit night. At this stage, I was excited to get going but despite what I'd experienced so far, I still had no real idea what was ahead for me.

The most physically and mentally demanding thing I have ever done in my life was just around the corner. I suspect it doesn't matter how many times or how in detail someone explains summit night to you, you'll never fully understand or believe it until you are there and doing it yourself. I suppose that could be said for anything and everything we do in life.

Before we left, we had a briefing. We would aim to reach Stella Point at 5am and the summit Uhuru Peak at 6.30am. Sunrise at the top of Kilimanjaro, that was the goal. With my many layers and head torch on, water bottles filled, walking poles and snacks packed, I was ready.

We left at 11pm.

The first two hours I felt fine, if anything, I was enjoying the scramble over rocks in the dead of the night with the guides singing in the background.

At first, I didn't understand the occasional instruction the guides interjected: *"wakey wakey, no sleeping"*, until suddenly, I did...

It's hard to fully explain the effects altitude had on my body and the level of fatigue I suddenly experienced on that last climb. First came the stomach cramps and headaches, then the drowsiness. I felt exhausted to the point of falling in and out of sleep, but to be woken by my guide, Marko, behind me.

For most of the climb, my body had no desire to move but my mind knew I had to. This is when my resilience kicked in. When it became more about my mindset than my physical strength. For five (long) hours, I dragged one foot in front of the other – over rocks and loose scree in the pitch dark head down staring only at my feet – with little on my mind but to 'keep going'. I knew we would be at Stella Point around 5am and just knowing that kept me motivated. I relied on Marko to keep me updated on the time (amongst many other things) as I physically couldn't go into my pocket to take out my phone and look. We took a break every hour but only for 5 minutes - which felt like seconds.

Marko was always by my side, observing the situation and always ready to jump in when I needed his help. He would take my rucksack off my shoulders and I would take a seat on a rock. By this stage eating and drinking was a struggle. Sitting lifeless on a rock Marko would rub my shoulders and legs to help release any tension and increase circulation, whispering *"good job"* while I forced myself to drink.

We arrived at Stella Point at 5.39am. Feeling exhausted, emotional, relieved and excited! As a group, we hugged, cried and congratulated each other for making it this far.

It felt like we had the worst behind us. We toasted with ginger tea, courtesy of our guides. But we didn't rest long as temperatures were well below freezing (-17 degrees!).

I'm not sure if it was the ginger tea, the hugs, the sun starting to rise or the fact I could finally see Uhura Peak (or maybe it was all four) but my spirits lifted and I got a second wind. I began to make my way towards the summit more mindfully and with ease.

This was my favourite part of the trek. Everything seemed so still and peaceful, there was hardly a word spoken as we walked by Kilimanjaro's stunning glaciers. The sun rising and the shadow of the mountain on the clouds was an incredible sight I won't soon forget. I walked to the top in awe and with great pride.. and then, I stood on the ***"Roof of Africa"*** at 6.36am on Friday 21st September 2023.

The summit was extremely busy, with crowds of people all wanting a photo with the famous Kilimanjaro sign (myself included!). There was even one gentleman making sushi—not at all what I was expecting! It felt like an overcrowded tourist attraction. Whether it was the exhaustion, the crowds of people or the fact that I still had to get down, it was almost hard to enjoy the moment. I had made it, the goal was reached and all I wanted to do was get down to camp and go to sleep.

As a group, we quickly got our photos and made our way down the scree slopes to the camp. This took around two hours.

Exhausted, dehydrated and feeling really rough we arrived back at camp to the nicest glass of pineapple juice. As others were still descending from the summit, a few of us sat around a table and shared our summit stories. I shared my experience with anger and frustration.

"Why did no one prepare us for that?"
"Why did we need to leave in the middle of the night?"

I wasn't alone in feeling these emotions but I was surprised by my reaction as it felt out of character. I can only assume this is normal — the intensity of the challenge, the lack of sleep and bottled up emotions that built during the night's trek, it's a lot. And after I got some sleep, had some time to process what had just happened and ate some good food, I felt better and I shared my story with the rest of the group in a different way, a less gloomy way. I was beginning to see the good in the struggle.

Once everyone got back to camp and had lunch, we then headed off on a four hour trek to our final camp on the mountain, Millennium Camp.

That night, we had dinner together and our guides presented us with a Kilimanjaro completion medal. It was a lovely way to end a long and gruelling day.

Leaving the mountain

Day seven. After the best night's sleep on the mountain, it was time to get up and pack my bag one last time. Before we left, we thanked the porters for their incredible help. Our trek would have been absolutely impossible without their support.

You cannot summit this mountain without them. Not only do they carry all the gear, do the cooking, keep you safe and guide you up the mountain, they do it all with the utmost kindness and compassion. Together, we sang and danced for the last time and took our final steps down the mountain.

Life after Kilimanjaro

Nobody ever talks about what happens when the adventure is over. When you're on the lonely journey back home, when you're falling right back into your everyday life. When everything is exactly how you left it and nothing has changed...but you.

It's tough. It took me a month to emotionally recover from my time on the mountain. I felt low and a bit lost. I missed my new friends and everything the mountain gave me - excitement, purpose and beauty. But I knew that was normal and to be expected, so I gave myself that time. I now look back and feel extremely grateful for everything that happened over that ten day opportunity.

Climbing Kilimanjaro was more than a trek up a mountain. It was an experience that taught me a lot about myself and my abilities. That I can dig deep when the going gets tough. That I can do hard things. But I discovered this about myself only by having the courage to move outside of my comfort zone. Outside our comfort zone is where growth happens. It's where we build the confidence to take on other challenges that we were once afraid to do. It's where future experiences will surely take me...and that's how I signed up to run the Paris Marathon in 2024!

Sarah Jane McGeown

The View I Didn't See
by Tabby Kerwin

Mount Kilimanjaro...

...the world's highest freestanding mountain and one of my greatest teachers to date. Between living with grief and climbing Kili I have learned so much about life, living, resilience, performance and gratitude.

I took my grief to the mountain with me... the losses of my Dad when I was 16-years-old, the death of my brother in 2014 and in 2018 the death of my husband Simon. They were heavy burdens to carry, but I carry that weight every day and went to the mountain expecting the enormity of it to give me some perspective. What I didn't count on was carrying past realities of mental health issues and eating disorders in my emotional backpack, but slowly over the week, each of these issues was unpacked in a fairly public release of emotions. Kili became my most honest teacher, my biggest challenge and my greatest therapist and I still look to her wisdom and lessons today.

My emotional backpack was heavy – but it was balanced with the immense joy and excitement ahead of the climb. I always knew it would test me to my limits but that thought never scared me—it excited me. The thought of meeting with 37 other trekkers who were strangers and undertaking this life-changing challenge alongside a huge supporting party of local Tanzanian experts never felt overwhelming. It just filled me with curiosity and excitement.

Since I randomly decided to undertake the challenge in January 2023, eight months before we departed, I was only ever filled with determination and a matter-of-fact attitude that said I was going to enjoy every moment of my adventure.

… and what an adventure it was – physically, spiritually, mentally and emotionally.

The biggest highlight of this adventure was the people with an array of personalities and characters, each with a different motivation for climbing, making up our group and the kindest, most supportive team of porters, guides and cooks. Without the people, this trip wouldn't have been nearly as memorable an experience; proving that connection is key to satisfaction, success and happiness.

The week was hard and when the basic requirements of sleep and food are not catered for in the way we have become comfortable with in our western lives, you find yourself checking your privilege and dealing with the emotional and physical impact of the truths you learn about yourself and your thinking. You only had to look around the people and lives of the local Tanzanian folk to bring yourself into check. The biggest asset they have is not money, property or power... it's a smile. They wear smiles with pride, they exude happiness and they lead with kindness and gratitude. It is humbling and the biggest lesson I took. Lead with your heart and everything else will follow.

I never doubted my physical or mental ability to climb Kilimanjaro—I knew it was more of a mental than physical game and my preparation factored this in. As a performance coach and a widow I knew my mental strength was pretty strong and could take another hammering and physically I'd put the work in—but honestly, no amount of preparation in the world prepares you for Kili. She is a formidable energy and physical presence and she keeps you guessing as to what challenge you will face next... will it be emotional or physical, spiritual or mental? Every moment of every day is different.

From a vast array of landscapes, weathers and terrains to the ever-changing air you breathe—physically you had to stay alert both day and night. Emotionally every step which you take *'pole pole'* (translating to slowly slowly) has to be mindful and having constant mantras and positive affirmations running through your head willing you to success, was often a must just to make the mind-body connection complete. I relied on those mantras to help me every step.

I may have had no-doubts in my preparation as to my ability to succeed, but from step one on day one of the climb, I realised exactly what a challenge it was going to be. It didn't matter how much preparation you had previously done, or how much you visualised your future goal, this climb required you to stay in the present moment constantly – and that can be a challenge in itself, because it is emotionally and physically painful.

Climbing Kilimanjaro is humbling. The mountain requires you to dig deep and she slowly unpacks your emotional baggage like an expert therapist – which, for me, was probably heavier than the physical backpack I was so grateful not to carry. On the mountain I truly learned how to check my ego, to welcome support and to allow myself to receive kindness. As a widow, single mum and solo business owner who lost her Dad when she was at school without the support she needed then, you become very independent—learning not to rely on anyone but yourself and reverting to stubbornness or self-sabotage as a form of protection. But Kili taught me it's safe to allow others in and that you don't have to carry all the physical and emotional burdens.

On the first few days I would feel bad about allowing a porter to carry my small backpack – *"I should be able to manage...others are...I will be stubborn and cope"* were thoughts running through my head, paralleled with another thought of *"but I really want the help but too ashamed to ask"*. Well, you learn the lesson quickly that accepting help is not shameful and it's not just OK, it's good and wise.

There is an African proverb that sprang to mind. **"If you want to go fast, go alone. If you want to go far, go together."**

I didn't want to go fast—I couldn't—the altitude and terrain didn't allow! But I did want to go far... and this meant accepting the support of others and setting down my FOPO (fear of people's opinions).

I was here for a reason. To undertake a mental and physical challenge, to raise awareness for grief and mental health of musicians (complete with my little blue plastic cornet tied to my backpack which was a great conversation starter as well as an alarm clock and part of the live entertainment for a side of the mountain rave!) and to learn about myself and other people.

Every day posed a new challenge. Physical ones, yes, but also emotional and mental ones. My ego was continually tested and set aside through leading groups because I had the slowest pace. This was a hard pill to swallow, because of the feelings of shame that come with it *'I'm the slowest'* but the only way to make it up this mountain is slowly, so actually it wasn't a judgement, it was a role I could play to support others... and that is always my purpose... to help others through the words I speak, work I do and actions I undertake. I was grateful when fellow climbers shared their relief at my pace setting because it helped them to feel better and as if they could complete the challenge. Slow was for the win on Kili.

Every day was hard, but there was always also joy. Day two offered my first experience of something that would ultimately lead to me not making it to the very top of Kili. I lost my ability to see anything. The world literally went black. My eyesight was gone in a flash. An uncommon side effect of altitude. It was a terrifying moment, yet I remained calm inside. This was a lesson from the mountain, another of her messages I had to listen to. Another discomfort I had to lean into. *"OK mountain, I'm listening—you've got my attention."*

Moments later my eyesight returned but it was hard to re-calibrate physical balance and emotions. A quick pit stop and then heading down the mountain a little to our camp for the night helped the eyesight, but there were so many mental questions at this stage. *Do I quit? Can I do this? What do I really want to achieve by being here?* The words rushed around my head.

I struggled to eat most days because of altitude and every part of my intelligence knew that I needed to eat for strength but eating made me physically sick and as someone who utilised Bulimia as a coping strategy for grief and sadness in her teenage years, the combination of being told to eat and past trauma was playing havoc with my mental state. So there, on the side of the mountain having momentarily lost my eyesight a few hours earlier, I unpacked that trauma and gave it up to the mountain. She took it from me, my emotional backpack now lighter and the next day I engaged my inner child for a fun day of climbing the Baranco Wall. One of the most difficult but fun challenges ever! I felt like a little mountain goat without a care in the world and I was away from the group as the guides thought it wise to give me time and space after the previous day and I left a little earlier ahead of the group with my guide Abdullah.

In hindsight I think they knew the emotional release I was going through and with that little space they gave me I got to have fun and not feel the pressure from others and that completely changed me. It meant that the next few days I was at ease going first, going slow, releasing FOPO and gradually I found a way to eat, without the shame of teenage Bulimic emotions. The mountain was powerful and the connections I built through conversations gave even more strength to all of us. The group was a set of individuals each undertaking and overcoming their personal challenges, yet collectively they were the most supportive and wonderful team, helping each other through kindness, gratitude, laughter, listening and song!

Day Five and moving from Karanga to base camp at Barafu and it seemed on waking the mountain decided I had built enough strength to face my next challenge... emotional challenge obviously... time to unpack some more emotional baggage and hand it over to her to safeguard.

The first hour was brutal followed by a few easier hours, but the last hour into base camp was really hard scrambling and as we went higher in altitude I started struggling with dizziness and a lack of vision again. But I made it to base camp, albeit it was a little bit blurry!

Tomorrow morning we would summit and that meant leaving base camp at 10pm. I had a small attempt at an afternoon nap but pre-departure things started to feel nerve-wracking. I spent two hours prior to departure with the positive mantra of "*I am strong, brave and capable*" running through my mind. Literally two hours of nothing but those words on repeat in my head. We set off and I knew straight away that something didn't feel right. The dizziness was getting worse with every movement and step by step my vision was going… going… gone.

I got a few hours in and to around 5500m but the dizziness was bad and I couldn't see a thing. Granted there wasn't a lot to see other than the stream of headtorches and a sky full of stars, but they had vanished from sight. My eyes were open but I couldn't see the faces in front of me.

Time to check my ego again because the default thought is *if I don't get that photo at the summit then people will think I've failed.* But this was not a failure. My intention was to climb Kilimanjaro and learn and grow, and my goodness, I'd done both in bucket loads – I didn't need a photo to prove it. So I tipped my ego off the mountain and did what was right and safe. The **Roof of Africa** may have been the view I didn't see that day, but I chose to see so many more views again in my future by not jeopardising my health and eyesight for the sake of ego. Thanks mountain. Lesson learned!

I returned to base camp to rest and await my new friends returning in the morning. Breathing is hard and whilst I can see again, albeit blurred vision, I can't help but reflect on my husband Simon's time in ICU before he died.

I'm grateful for the lessons I learned from the physios there helping him to breathe because their advice helped me in that moment, but those thoughts of Simon brought a whole wave of sadness and emotion and grief and the tears flooded out of me for the next six hours. Clearly a release the mountain knew I needed which left me refreshed and ready to welcome everyone back and share in their joy and pain and support them all in the way that they needed.

The final day of climbing arrived and I hoped by this point that the hardest lessons Kili had to give were done with... but I was wrong. The final day would be an early start and a 13.5km walk – all downhill! It was brutal. Physically by far the worst pain in your knees and legs and after seven hours without stops I made it to the end point – behind everyone else, alone (aside from the few guides who generously stayed with me) and utterly broken.

That downhill stretch was, for me, the scariest part. It triggered my fears of falling, it was painful and I cried with every step. There were moments I truly believed I could not go one step more, but I did thanks to the support of my amazing guides. I beat shame as people went past me, I battled with my own mind but I got there and just like living with grief, I did it my way.

Grief is like a mountain; it's never straight up and down and there is a challenge and test at every moment. But if you connect with the right people, if you embrace and listen to the lessons, you can move through the discomfort to become stronger.

Kilimanjaro may have offered the view I didn't see, but the mountain and the people offered me the lessons and healings I didn't know I needed, for which I am so grateful.

Would I do it again? In a heartbeat.

Why? Because of the people—not just those in my group, but the people of Tanzania who lead with their hearts, with kindness, gratitude and happiness.

Kili changed me. She was my greatest challenge, my greatest teacher and by far my greatest therapist!

Tabby Kerwin

Ready for the off!

(L-R) Kissing the Baranco Wall, life above the clouds &
the amazing porters at work

(Top L-R) Adrian, Emma, Jo & her husband Paul

(Top L-R) Karen, Lee & Lily

(Top L-R) Rich, Sarah Jane, Tabby

Printed in Great Britain
by Amazon